SAYLESSI SAVANT

From my
mind to
yours...
ENJOY

A DECADE OF CURATED POEMS
MINDMOTIF MEDIA

Paperback ISBN: 979-8-218-44795-3

Library of Congress Number: TXu 2-418-125
First paperback edition February 2024.
Editing, Cover Art And Layout By
Saylessi Savant

Produced by

Mind Motif Media

Dedication

To my brothers and sisters of the Pen: Your unwavering support and guidance have been instrumental in shaping my craft over the years. Your creative investment will always be cherished, and the refinement you brought to my poetry will never be forgotten. Thank you.

To my Mom: Though you are not here to read this, I know you would be proud that I followed through on the vision we shared. Thank you for opening my eyes to the many ways of seeing the world. I will see you on the other side.

To Mek: From day one, you believed in me when no one else would. Your dedication, sacrifices, and unwavering support have been the foundation of this creative journey. I will never forget the strength you gave me. Thank you.

To my beloved children: This is a piece of me that will endure forever. Whenever you need to, you can find me within these words.

Angled Table Of Contents

Preface

 This collection of poetry traverses the often tumultuous terrain of human existence, painting vivid images with words that cut to the bone and heal the soul. Each poem is a reflection of the struggle, the pain, the triumphs, and the profound moments of introspection that define our shared humanity.

You will meet a soul battling it's inner demons and external adversities, wrestling with identity, and striving to find peace amidst chaos. The poet's voice, at times tender and at times fierce, guides you through a world where hope and despair coexist, where dreams are both a refuge and a battlefield. The themes of faith, resilience, and transformation echo throughout, reminding us that even in our darkest hours, there is a spark of light waiting to be ignited.

This collection does not shy away from the harsh truths of our world. It challenges the reader to confront uncomfortable realities, to empathize with the pain of others, and to find solidarity in shared struggles. It is a testament to the power of words to both wound and heal, to both imprison and liberate.

Prepare to be moved, to be challenged, and to be inspired. These poems are not just words on a page; they are a call to action, a plea for understanding, and a celebration of the indomitable human spirit. Let them wash over you, let them provoke thought and stir emotion, and most importantly, let them remind you of the beauty and strength that lie within us all.

Welcome to a world where the personal becomes universal, where the poetic becomes political, and where every line is a testament to the enduring power of the human heart.

With heartfelt gratitude to my poetic mentor and creative godmother, Deborah Tabola. Thank you for seeing the light in us when society saw only darkness, for helping us reclaim our humanity, and for revealing the power of our voices. I will forever be grateful for the wisdom and inspiration you poured into us. Now, we have something beautiful to share with the world.

Saylessi Savant
06/19/2024

let it be said let it be done

The Process of the Process

A Dollar Short

"Excuse me sir I'm hungry can you spare some..."
Sorry, but you're a Dollar Short!
"My wife really needs the emergency procedure...
Hun?- No I don't have insurance, but..."
A Dollar Short!
"Yes I'm a little behind on bills, but
my kids need lights and gas, it's winter and..."
A Dollar Short!
"I lost my legs for this country.
I'm a little behind on rent can I please"
A Dollar Short!
God sent the offering plate back around and said
"I'm a Dollar Short"
Millions die every year of starvation
because they are
A Dollar Short!
With a state-appointed lawyer: 15 years
With a paid lawyer: 3 months and a drug program
Justice said I was
A Dollar Short!
Beneath the poverty line, I'm...
$5 short of ultra-wealthy
A Dollar Short of poverty.
A Dollar Short of working class.
A Dollar Short of middle class.
A Dollar Short of the upper class.
A Dollar Short of wealthy.
I would be recognized as a human being, but
I'm a Dollar Short!

A Wife's Last Wish

I remember when I could laugh
before my lungs filled with fluid.
I used to speak my mind freely
before the hiss of oxygen tubes drowned me out.
I was transparent, like the plastic mask
that now muffles my voice.
But at least, at least,
you can read my lips.
Are you reading them? Look closely...
I love you.
So, when I go,
cry for me with tears of joy,
for I won't suffer anymore.
I'm more aware now
of the circle of life.
I see the white light...
no, wait—
that's just how bright
I always knew you were.
I don't see this as leaving you behind,
but leading you to the next phase of life
without me.
I'm free—finally—so be happy.

Alone Finally

I haven't walked barefoot in over eight years.
Sand grains wrestle for position between my toes,
nature's first Dr. Scholl arch support, comforted by its
grooves,
walking the tidal line of moist and dry,
a coastal balance beam.

I finally have the freedom to hear myself think.
My only influence: me, an oceanic breeze, and
understanding aloneness in this universe, yet at the same
time
deeply in tune
to the weave of
one with everything, connectivity.
Seaweed tags me on the feet
as the tide recedes,
life getting my attention.
Solitude is intentional,
isolation involuntary.
The former is what
the fruit of my peace has been birthed from.

Wrestling with the residue of a chaotic life,
my mind reacts to phantom traumas of past regret,
while paradise is before me.
It's trying to reject the actuality of this space, hardened
responses.

I stumble onto shipwrecked debris:

13

chapstick, a cracked iPhone, a gold chain tangled in fishnet.
My shoreline monastery encroached upon by worldly objects.
I guess the speedboat saw the lighthouse, but not the rocks.

I make a crude sandcastle with a high enough
bank to prevent erosion from tides,
thinking, "I should have done this more with my son"
when he was a child,
safeguarding us from the erosion of time on our bond.

I feel like I'm reintroducing myself to me,
like I've been wearing tons of costumes
and pounds of makeup.
The social accessories that I felt made me up,
I guess I thought I needed crutches
when I was naturally a good runner.

I find myself checking my thoughts
to not spoil this visual and spatial bliss before me.
I'm done thinking just for the sake of thinking,
I just want to feel for the sake of feeling.

Tried emptying myself into a state of just being,
but the nothingness fights with me to fill the void,
with stuff for the sake of having stuff going on,
AKA busybody syndrome.

I haven't run and just leapt as high as I can in a while,
nor shouted at the top of my lungs without
being perceived as crazy, or
gone swimming naked and air-dried
under the sun.

I think I'll do that now.

Meditate for a while, while my eyes open
out to this beautiful world
that someone either considered hell on earth
or a visual reference to heaven.

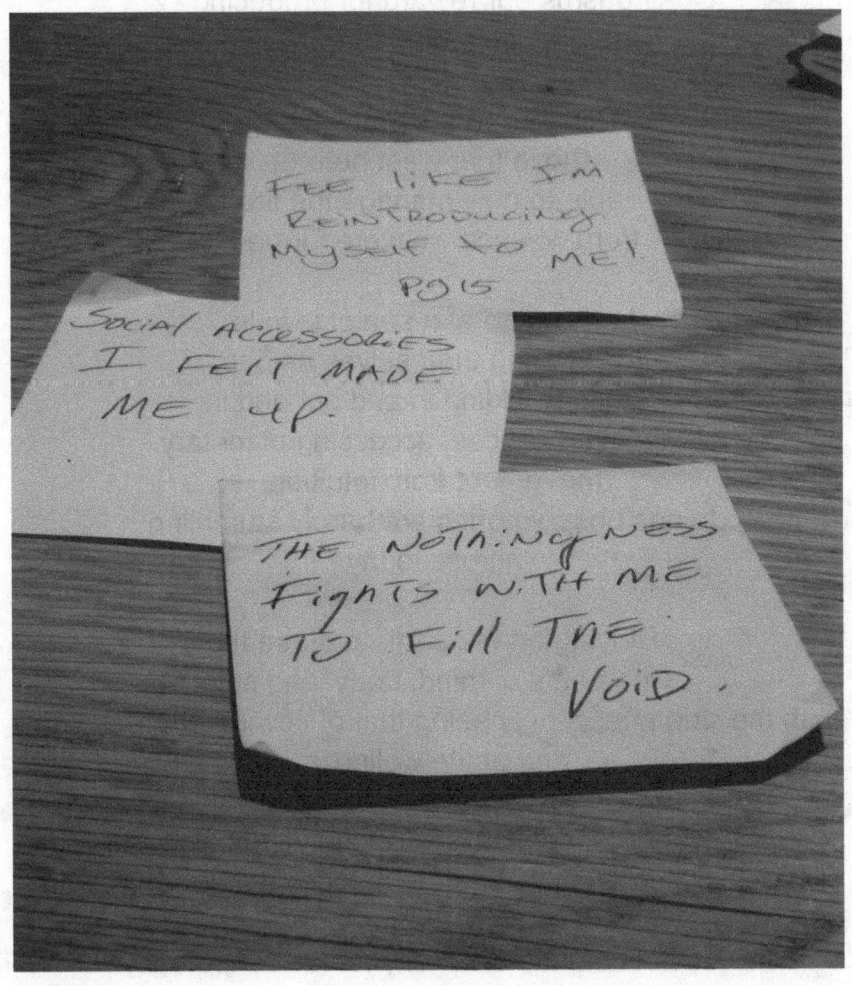

Ancestral Spiral

Emerging from a cosmo-gasm,
fire weaving our organic tapestry 23.
Orgasms our reward for producing
more of life's Representatives.

Walking art forms, my ancestors,
those that went before,
able to now manage the fire
from whence we were formed.

Looking up at a sea of jewels,
considering themselves as one,
our life twinkling in and out and in.
Mapping the skies, accessing planetary
movement from intuition,
things observatories are barely stumbling
across today.

Relying on the earth to nurse the
alignments of mind, body, and spirit,
with the side effects only being that of flowing appreciation,
and acute wellness.

Physicians, spiritualists, and psychologists—
terms only separate in today's age.
A unified art form.
Let's not confuse simplicity for lack of potency.

They were pre-programmed to be in harmony with nature's
balance;

sustainability was instinctual,
thanking each life form consumed.

Communal justice and civic responsibility,
maintained through tribal agreements.
Responsible with their words,
tongue kept pure for the sanctity
of their oral traditions.
Gossip was rewardless.
Vocal vibratory songs soothed the mind
of both new soul in cradle
and mature one on night watch.

Soles of feet massaged by the roughage of moist red soil,
dancing ecstatically from
the rare occasion that music
entrances them,
allowing
their vessels to be housed by those that went before them.

Filled with their spirits: One with all.
Death not perceived as such,
but rather a spirit's return to the fire
it emerged from,
and the remaining body a gift to the Earth
for other life forms to say thank you

" *Artist Pen*"

My magic wand, my sword, my therapist—
a prescription for a depressive condition,
abracadabra materializing well-thought-out intentions.
Overlooking jagged-edge cliffs invaded by a legion of poppy
flowers,
it's beautiful how my mind blooms and words pollinate
mindscapes.
Word choice begins with internal voice;
I consider its hymn, project death or life.
Responsibility acknowledged from distributor to recipient.
My pen could declare war that would last for eons,
or suggest a peace we wish to immerse in.
If the transmission of ideas
is sharpened with each successive work,
slicing complacency off of lean thought,
decapitating rosebuds that
are non-yielding.
A mirror image of flourishing won't cut it,
being productive,
a contributor to something greater
than what I think I see.
Like an ink splash interpretation
psychoanalyzed
by one who can see sound,
hear peppermint,
or taste blues in an emotional hue.
My pen is the pill prescribed for maladies of the spirit,
a soft garment in case my outlook on life hardens.
Allow me to sew it to my heart,
so that I may never relapse

into
not expressing myself ever again,
and having the courage to entertain
the thoughts of being crucified by critics,
yet resurrecting with something
I didn't know yesterday.
Helping others ascend in what I may communicate today,
moving by
the empowerment of a free-flowing
breeze of inspirational wind,
flying kites, paragliding to free falling,
landing en route with a zip-line.
This is written light from a bioluminescent mind

Busy Living Focused

Refrained from talking on an unscheduled notice.
"Get it! Get it! Get it!"
Scrawled across my daily planner
with a message that self-destructs.
Cremating the faulty thinking and illegible moments
of previously doubting myself on yellow post-its.
Taming the hobgoblin of distraction from within the lotus
by dreaming internationally
while mastering local motives.
Proclaiming the mantra: "I am Unstoppable,"
reverting the German swastika back to its intended purpose
of a peace offering,
but only if my actions proceed with focus.
Can't take appearance seriously.
A smile could be the route to any given conspiracy.
I'd rather chew on spiritual truths with the missing tooth,
than show that my veneers are pristine under the guillotine.
Empirical evidence is dear to me.
Cardiologic: Get into the heart of the matter and
disregard the outer clothing.
Rather listen to hints of truth within men
struggling to express themselves in a desire to be open.
Within you is a granted fortress of uniqueness,
please protect the solid from erosion... you need this.
Learn to thaw out trauma that has been frozen
in internalized moments,
being real with yourself as to where you went left,
because no man in his right mind will refuse a right action
after his mind has provoked him.

You see, I learned that the foulest thing that comes from a
man
is not waste or fluids from illness,
but rather when a sick heart discharges
psychological bile,
especially when he loses it.
Like tiptoeing through an avalanche crash course yo-ledi-
dooing,
with a bitter prenatal crack soul the '80s influence.
Grown and sophisticated, but I survived some costly
mistakes.
A hard head makes a whooped ass for talking back to life
like moms,
until she responds, "boy, up off you, I'll beat them brakes."
Saving my life with pain being inflicted,
wet and naked being whipped out of love, no hate within it.
But on this road to success, seat belts and tire pressure
don't always ensure the safest trip.
A few times I crashed with defective airbags
and choked on windshield glass.
I apologized, but a response might take some time.
Forgave myself and
decided to fly instead of drive.
Appreciating the wisdom of humility through being tried.
I used the pressure of conformity to burst through my fears of
being original
and make people gravitate towards my standard bar,
encouraging them to
pull
up
calisthenically with their own spin on it.
Tucking forgotten memories of pain like photo albums under
basement bricks,
swallowed the challenging pill of greatness

21

to acquire its traits and make it stick,
just to put sapphire, diamonds, and wisdom on my daughter's
neck and bracelet

Perspective

Living in a world where
the truth is on the decline,
mud on boots,
bullet casings, blood, and body parts.
"Those were good recruits."
The barrel recoils,
the spoils of war a barrel of oil,
common knowledge.
Either we are double-minded or
our guilty conscience is giving us brownies
to shut up.
It's not that the conscience is guilty
but sees and speaks clearly,
truth unfiltered,
just like a child,
"sit down now and hush" we say, "stay out of grown folks'
business,"
knowing everything at the
expense of those that need
not words or charades to showboat,
but turning in a lease of faith in exchange
to one day own hope.

Contrast

Shadows fall where light stands up,
fire sits where smoke dances.
Peace is a struggle's aftereffect,
love is hate's alter ego.
A cold heart is a corpse's signature,
a warm feeling is life's appreciation for itself.
The truth is a lie's interdependent arch-nemesis,
while strength is only weakness on a good day.
A smile is but a frown's reflection.
We are all but criminals that haven't been exposed yet
in somebody's court of self-righteousness,
judgment of bias, misinformation, and prejudice.

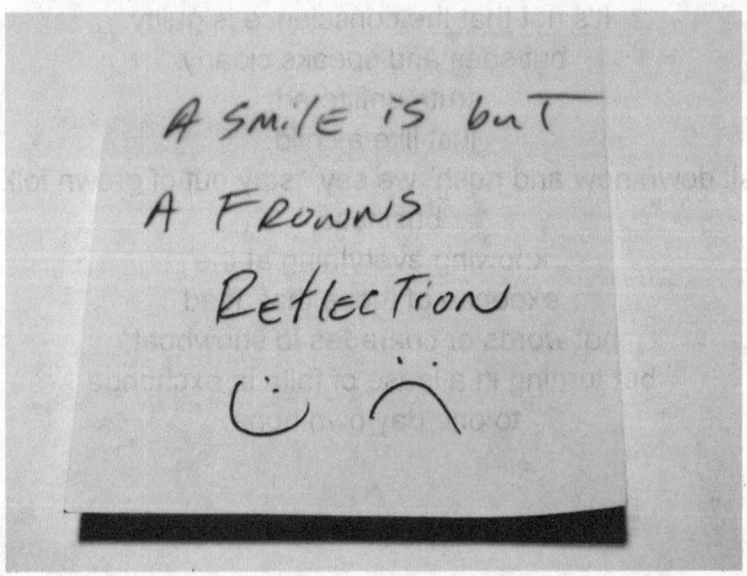

Deep Dive

I'm desperately trying to find my higher self
in a world of lowly consideration.
Frivolously searching every nook and cranny
in a forgotten place,
damp with the tears of unseen, sobbing faces,
and littered with the still-wet surgical gauze from
unsuccessful dissections
of my irrational beliefs.

I became infected with impatience.
My traumas are cryogenically frozen,
in suspended animation.
Contained within a falsely labeled, shatter-proof vial of denial
that's sensitive to temperature changes.
Hence, the bipolarity of my nature.

Or is it simply that I've been exposed to emotional extremes?
Happiness and hate in my life,
shootings at birthday parties,
new job yet more bills,
falling in love, yet hating myself,
witnessing both births and murders on the same day.
Free but enslaved by the pursuit
of escaping my have-nots.
My pain is contagious, but I'm not ashamed to admit that.
I need a hug.
One of those moms used to give.
Warm, tight, snug—genuine.

25

Yeah, one of those.

I've employed reverse psychology to counteract the
intentions of my pain,
which was to make others feel the pain that I have been
issued,
but I refuse.
Instead, I identified the very thing that's killing them slowly—
the thing I know all too well.
Revealing my wounds just to demonstrate how to stitch them
closed,
a symbolic gesture of hope.

This is how you take those vicious blows
while your back is against those ropes.
Everybody is waiting for the moment when
your chin shatters and your body drops
limp to the floor, blindly grasping with stiff outstretched arms
seeking to regain the sense of security you once had.
Obsessively "what if" drunk on the punch you never got to
throw.

Yes, they were waiting on that, believe it or not,
but you didn't drop.
The pain that they wanted you to succumb to,
they are now stuck with because,
the smile on your face disgusts them.

Their outlook on life,
their predictions about you,
their hoping for you to fail,
dashes against the rocks like a mishandled child

not supervised at the Grand Canyon.
You shattered their reality by exhibiting grit
that they would never possess or think was even possible.

Yeah, you show them. No!
You showed yourself,
because you needed to know what you could do,
and who you could trust through life's tests.

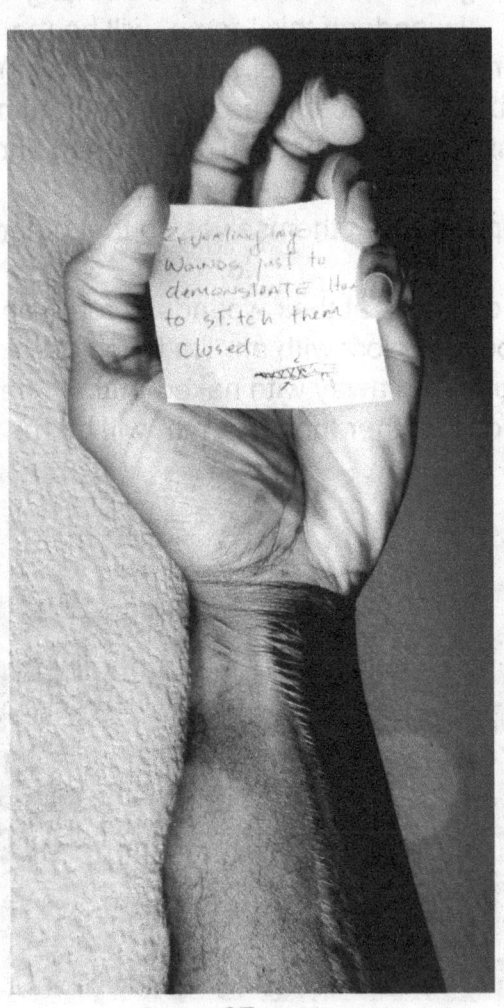

Exclusive

Some people smoke on black bile
to have brighter days.
Some people are lunatics without a full moon.
Some will sell their soul but won't accept refunds.
Some give birth to doubt while aborting dreams.
I wonder if this "some" will be me.
Some will say, "Never second-guess yourself,
but rather do it three or four more times
just to be sure that you're confused and lost
like the rest of us."
Some people stare at themselves so that others won't have
to.
Some people pick at their wounds to remember the pain.
Some are lost with an "I'm found" t-shirt on.
Some run away with naked truths... naked.
I question whether those "some" will be me one day?

Fatal Attraction

Swept off my feet by
a one-sided lover.
I didn't have to pretend to be someone else
to be accepted
with my pre-existing conditions.
You traveled over a thousand miles,
by hitchhiking, just to reach me.
You took my breath away.
Changed my life
and the world as I know it.
I have splitting headaches and a dry mouth.
Sense of smell and taste erased.
This is becoming abusive.
I thought the affection was exclusive,
but a million others have already had you.
It seems like you've been faithful to many,
not just me.
One-tenth of them could actually
live without you,
but you didn't let them live for very long
to find out.
I feel like something is obstructing my PPE,
waiting to exhale.
I can no longer speak—I wheeze.
It's you, isn't it!?
Heartache—warmth—darkness—cold

Floating Wishes

I have never seen a falling star in the afternoon,
bright with a smoke trail streaming across the sky.
I close my eyes and wish for world peace,
not wishing for more because this should satisfy all.
This falling star is different in that it hasn't
lost its flicker as it approached the smoggy city.

Living in the hills is the envy of the city.
The fog would look like a sea of clouds in the morning, but
turn into mud by noon.
Thick exhaust from commuters chasing happiness and they
haven't stopped running.
Chem-trail X marks the spot of God's arrival from the sky.
My mom used to say, but now she's saying nothing at all.
An emergency broadcast blares from the TV, cell phone, and
air-quality shattering my peace.

60 pills washed down, my mom kissed me, cried, and found
her peace.
The falling star struck the city.
A red, molten marble mushroom is destroying everything.
I didn't hear the wrath of the falling star of noon
until 8 seconds after the fire licked the sky.
Thrumm! The heat came after, making my skin boil, but the
infinity pool hasn't.

I jumped into the water thinking it would cool the burns, but it
hasn't.

Underwater, the view of clouds is like thick black rolls of ink,
no longer peaceful.
My imagination comforts me. The darkness is the ground,
and I'm floating in the sky.
Should I descend from heaven to inhale the fumes of the
burning city?
Or should I inhale here, returning to the water, forgetting the
wish of noon?
Would anyone miss me, or is there anyone left to miss me at
all?

Was my wish not specific enough? A sinister genie thought
peace meant killing all.
You would think technology would improve the human
condition, but it hasn't.
Just because life has failed me, I won't fail it. I emerge at 15
minutes past noon.
My eardrums are bleeding, and I can't hear the sound effects
of the carnage around me. Peace.
The hills are no longer envied; they are equally tainted with
the city.
Three more falling stars cut through the scorched sky.

Three wishes for me; the first one would be to vacuum the
sky,
back to blue.
The second would be to give my mom hope not to want to
end it all.
And remove the fire chewing on the city.
I open my eyes, wishing things had changed, but they
haven't.

One of the shooting stars is falling my way. I raised two fingers for peace.
It's as bright as the sun at noon.
I thought this would change my mind about peace, but it hasn't.
My soul disintegrates into the sky. Finally... Peace.
Before a new day comes, the evening does after noon.

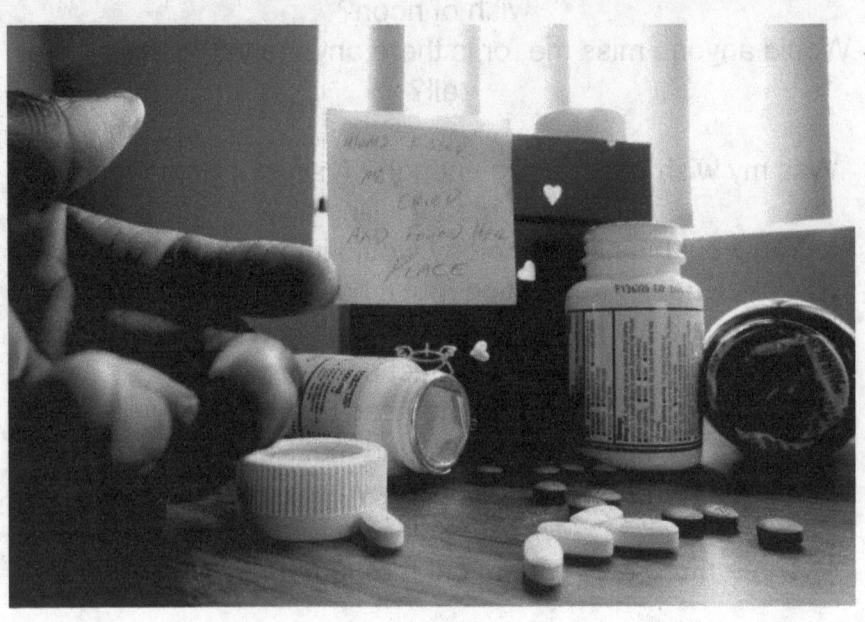

I In My Items

Holy, yet worn down
and still warm in this cold world,
like when my big toe pokes
through my sock.
Sturdy thoughts,
yet dirty and greased like my wave cap.
I mean "thinking cap."
It's tied before I sleep
and intact when I rise early.
My intuition was tried and tested,
yet it offers protection like my work gloves,
saving me from deep cuts and burns.
I've been through some tough times:
dirt, glass, pebbles, and spit.
But still fresh like my sneakers—Air Force Ones.
My posture is presidential.
Even bright days are shaded depending on life,
like my sunglasses.
I've been judged, sympathized with, admired, praised, and
demonized.
What an emotional roller coaster my brilliant and flawed
decisions took me through.
Except I don't scream when falling; I just brace myself
and get on the ride again.
Once it's over, my heart tick-tocks like my watch.
We both run on batteries and have two hands to praise space
with,
hiding scars, insecurities, and shame behind tailor-made

I Hear You Finally

Angry screams.
Hysterical laughter.
Pants and moans under soft music.
Birds chirp and Twitter message notifications ping.
All on the canvas of the eardrum.
Like a waterfall or dynamite ignited.
The soda pop can tops hiss.
A whisper:
"I don't think I can do this anymore."
A roar.
Coachella readings peak.
I listen to you until I can't.
An unintentional intention
when it hurts to listen.
Your apologies are like pebbles skipping off a heart of stone.
Silence.
Tears on the pillow,
sobbing and accompanied by muffled breathing,
rapid thuds of the heart.
The slam of a door,
car keys jingle,
tires rolling on pavement.
A song is playing:
Keyshia Cole's
"I Don't Love You No More."
Both the engine and song fade into the distance.
Wind ruffling through porch chimes,
basketball bouncing,

dog barking, window closes.
Silence.
Knees are popping,
the bed springs crunch,
tick-tock goes the clock,
nose sniffling tears and snot.
Pen rolling on paper.
Shoebox lid falls on carpet,
tissue paper ruffles.
A box falling on the ground.
Revolver hammer cocked.
Teeth chattering on metal.
Throat swallows saliva and tears.
"Dad, what are you doing?"
is heard.
"Dad, no! Put the gun down. What are you doing?"
She's right. What am I thinking?

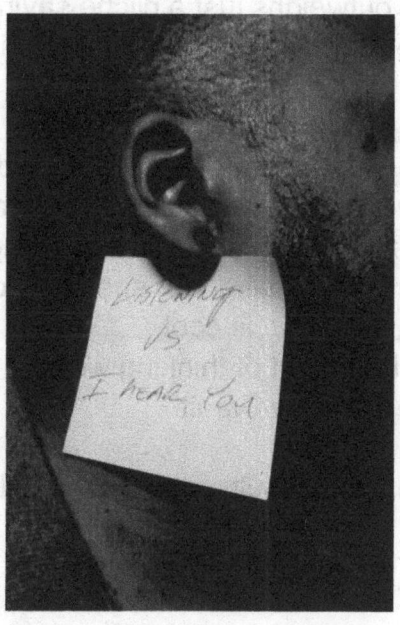

I Value Me

The value of a diamond in a box
doesn't depreciate just because it's locked.
The visionary in me sees beyond what's perceived to be lost.
The gun tower and razor wire dissolve,
as long as my purpose is involved.
Considering myself an asset
with a non-shoddy report,
while making amends for the faults that I was responsible for.
Society can't referee the ascendency of my self-esteem.
Had to sidestep the cousin of death,
self-loathing and its disease.
Like going on a sleazy date with a cheapskate player,
actually loving yourself
far outweighs just a cliché saying.
The estimation of my value requires
complicated tools.
Better have an infinite loop
on whatever measuring tape you decide to use.
The way I move, put my mind to use captivates the room.
Came from either billions of years of being fine-tuned
or I'm the result of God using "its" specialty tools, either way
is cool.
I'm going to make the art of thinking well the new symbol of
wealth.

Actions—results, actions—results,
for lack of better words,
let it speak for itself.

Because the chances of my being alive and through all
the bullshit I survived,
I'm walking astronomical odds.
My mold broke the cookie cutter.
My uniqueness cannot be robbed.
I was choking on self-deception until it was dislodged.
The truth heimliched my diaphragm,
I smiled and responded in kind, and
sipped from its fountain of wisdom.
You could be someone's stepping stone,
or have the mindset to elevate beyond convention.
Don't want to be one that's
among those who died in their indecision
and never distinguishing the line between
having life and bullshit twisted.
I had to clear out the pollutants
to realize that I was exclusive.
The result of work, effort, and facts,
removed safe from delusions.
The formula of all the greats
that arrived at the same conclusion.
Drink water for hiccups, become empowered from stigmas.
I refuse to live another man's lie,
or inhale the stench of the narrative he whiffs up.
But it would stick if I was ignorant enough.
My lifelong goals overshadow these temporary cuffs.
I canceled my subscription to the network of victimhood.
Leave the ground where it's at; heights are misunderstood

Intrepid Journeys

First name: Stressed the f*** out.
Last name: Worried.
Basking once again in skewed realities,
as you can see,
the intricate weaves of denial patterns
checkered on my past and life jacket.
Concerning?
Nah, numbing myself and having the nerve
to gloat about the bells and whistles
of dysfunction associated with it.
I never thought a lie could be a safety vest.
The cold truth at 30 degrees below zero could
turn warm hearts blackened by frostbite.
How am I doing?
Oh, fine!
Saying I'm okay yet my world is crumbling,
like smelling the roses with an infected sinus
and putting on a fake smile saying,
"The fragrance is earthy and sweet."
Entirely constructed from memory,
drowning in the past, hands of time tied up,
quicksand chained to my feet.
The placebo effect isn't working with my wishful thinking.
Like wearing a flimsy, perforated mask
in a gas chamber or room saturated with COVID.
A psychological comfort in knowing that I have one at least.
Wait! Why don't you have yours on?
I have an award for being
"The best at not acknowledging my bullshit,"

pinned on my hypothetical shoulder.
Meanwhile:
scorched earth, battle-pockmarked craters,
bloated bodies and dark, weeping skies.
PTSD as well as CTSD - Post and Current
Traumatic Stress Disorder
from the warfare in my mind.
Walking to and fro, yet
feeling buried alive
with a depressive disease
armed to the teeth and ready to kill me.
Yet hope is the chest harness that braces me
from my free-fall canyon dive belly flop.
Tears hitting the jagged edge rocks
instead of me, I **see**
a delayed reflection of myself in the mirror,
body jerking from life's
subsonic hollow-point rounds.
A puppeteer with Parkinson's
rocking my bulletproof mentality,
but what I think of myself doesn't prevent bruising,
shock, and internal bleeding
from the blunt force.
Enter the optimistic me again saying,
"Well, it could always be worse."

It's A Mans World

The ego screams and points at an optical illusion,
a contorted, disproportionate view
of man's place in the world.
Vision funneled, grasping power with an
arthritic hand, pulling puppet strings
with blistered fingers and carpal tunnel.
It's like watching a statue mourn,
a crying shame with cemented tear ducts.
We look you in the eye so that we can hide
the K-9 smiles of our lies.
Attempt to read through the blurred lines
or hear what you want.
We don't know everything most of the time.
Stone-faced, yet shivering from the
cold truth boxing inside.
Cowering behind appearance.
Marble hearts match the monuments of our pride.
While the pigeon droppings—
green, white, and brown semi-liquid poop—
run down the cheek of our memorials as a memoir.
"To us, an achievement; to them, a stoop."
Not counting the verbal assaults,
stranger spittle, and pebbles thrown by passersby
pinging off the metal plaque
written by nature.
As a reminder that
we are not in control of anything
that could be built with our hands and idolized with our mind.

The loudest statements at times are muted.
Our intellect is only a thick and creamy
pool of regurgitated instances of thought
produced and remembered by a select few.
Speaking and thinking in, "as you tell it,"
yet we dream like dogs,
eat like cows,
blink like camels,
and mate like hogs.
Savages with table manners.
War, lust, kill—
bestial animals that pant from
the exhaustion of pursuing innate highs
like a child attempting to catch a hummingbird.
Naturally observing the commandments in reverse:
Kill, steal, lie, covet everything that belongs to your neighbor,
and
depend on everything that is subservient to us, hmm.
Imagine that.
It's a man's world, but
we are dependent on the very things that we think are
subservient to us.
We are nothing but animated bags of blood, bones, and bile.
The arrogant stench of primal lust
repulses our higher self,
so we drench it in Hugh Hefner's cologne.
Supposed masters of the universe but rather
unique, logically conditioned civic beasts.
Heavenly-minded in the animal kingdom,
but "it will be nothing, nothing,"
without woven social construction of
Lego-blocked biased beliefs,
glued on top of wicker baskets.

Whisked together with multiple personality disorders,
whistle reeds declaring the value of a thing.
$500,000 for a watch, but
$1 a month for a starving child
with flies crawling into and out of each orifice—ears, eyes,
and mouth?
While the windows of the soul gloss over with a question,
"Can you empathetically become like one of these in a man's
world?"

Journey Glimers

A million and one,
swimming seeds,
first place won.
Fertilized eve—divided multiplicity.
Heartbeat, belly gel, and me on screen they see.
Aware of my feet, and when moms would sing.
She screamed, I could breathe.
Dropped by accident,
high gravity,
steps wobbly but balanced.
I cry and then get things,
I can now speak and on my own eat.
Training wheels off, ramps I'm hopping off.
Kissed a girl—warm—tingly.
Had a fight. Anger—fear—nervousness.
"He started it. Why don't you believe me?"
My lungs burning, I'm choking, eyes red,
hungry... everything's funny.
Keys to the car.
Diploma.
Liquor license.
Club scene.
It's getting hot in here.
Some say the X makes the sex spectacular.
Drunk in love, DUI—jail—times hard.
Baby on the way.
Lost job, found a mask—quick cash, and I'm a rapper at that.
Studio vices—nose burning—throat drip.
Chasing dragons or

girls tatted with one.
Unfaithful. Heartbreak. Sleepless nights.
Lost mind, dark crash.
Sentenced to a concrete box,
a million steps paced in an 8x10.
Found my mind; helped others find theirs.
Accepted errors, made amends.
Picked up a pen, now I'm here.

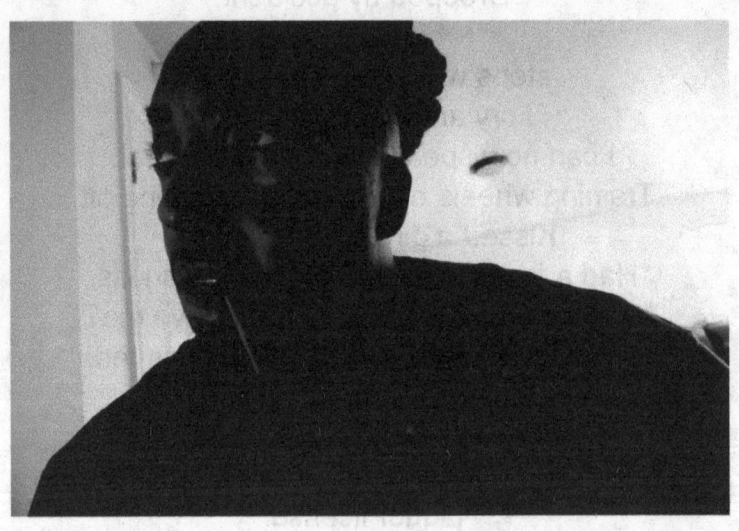

La Pluma Pen

With a slight bend,
I'm hard-pressed,
simply because of someone else's fear
of slipping and making an error.
I could work well without the pressure,
but his need for control
won't let me just flow,
but rather place a constrictive
strain on the core of my being,
for his expression.
I mean... I'm built for the task
but I enjoy being utilized
by the more
gracious and finesse-full.
I do understand moments of passion,
like when someone uses me to communicate with others,
or moments when one really needs to make a strong
statement,
but to those who have a continued grip
on my neck, a little advice:
Just loosen up on the pen when you write,
just a little bit, I'm not going anywhere.

Labels, Light, Leaves, Lens, Labels, Let, Life, Labor.

Be willing to revise your
labels,
observe the hue of green,
a rejected
light wave of color
that the
leaves reflected and didn't accept.
We see; therefore, we think
that the trees'
leaves are green.
The tree says, "No, they are not."
But we insist.
Because changing the meaning of our observation will require
a thorough revision of what we thought we were taught.
The attribute of a thing is what we believe it to be.
So, shine your
light of justice with care.
Too little light—not enough energy for growth.
Too much light causes overexposure and leads to dryness.
The heat from the light gives birth to fire,
a fire that affects everyone in the habitat.
The same with the riotous effects of people overburdened by
the light of justice.
Too little: lawlessness.
Too much: oppression and abuse of power,
leading to revolt.
So, listen carefully:

A baby cries for its mother inside a hot car.
Protesters at the capitol,
the truly innocent strongly debated as guilty,
pleading their case from behind bars to their captors.
The sound of a tree falling in the forest,
easier to identify than the three previously mentioned.
So let the mineralized tears of experience
seep and speak to the root of your issues.
Drink more from the storms of life to replenish your depleted
reservoir.
The fruit of your labor will spoil if not harvested,
or maybe perceived as ripe for the picking in appearance,
but with an inner worm burrowing tunnels.
Make your heart a home for your thoughts and beliefs,
but watch your guests
and the cancerous and parasitical company they keep.
Oversee these matters with the wisdom of an old tree.

47

Light House Duty

Lighthouse duty helped me find myself,
from my own torrential storms and sea salt-filled lungs.
I was being strangled by the rope of lack of hope,
a queued interlude for healthy vicissitudes.
My laughter was actually just a very well-disguised death
gurgle.
Glad to be sober with a revived mind,
instead of my purpose and potential being torn in two.
I didn't realize I needed this,
had been with festering wounds for so long,
I made them fashionable.
Being enabled by society's slogan of
"Toxicity is the New Normal,"
thought I had good footing on solid ground
until my earthquake brought down my tower of
disillusionment.
My inner man's ashen hand,
twitching out from the twisted rebar and collapsed concrete.
I can now see distress signals,
because I became aware of mine.
Have you ever seen someone drowning with a smile on their
face?
That was me at one time.
Contemplating my immortality:
this ocean, this lighthouse, these breaker stones
were here before I viewed them,
but I would like to think I was somewhere prior to these.

Not fearing the "living while dying" paradox of my life cycle.
Every time I excel, eternity becomes more vibrant.
My present fades into the past when I blink.
Everything new becomes old before you can say "new."
Do we have to go through trials and pain to reach paradise?
Or be the fittest to survive just to die?
I would love to see the movie of life from beginning to
endgame.
Observing my shadow's silhouette as the sun sets,
"Who is that man?" the shadow says and I flinch.
"Who, me? I'm just getting around to finding out."
Reconfiguring myself in the soup of my cocoon,
with good karmic gestures, trickle-down blessings,
and positive butterfly effects that ripple.

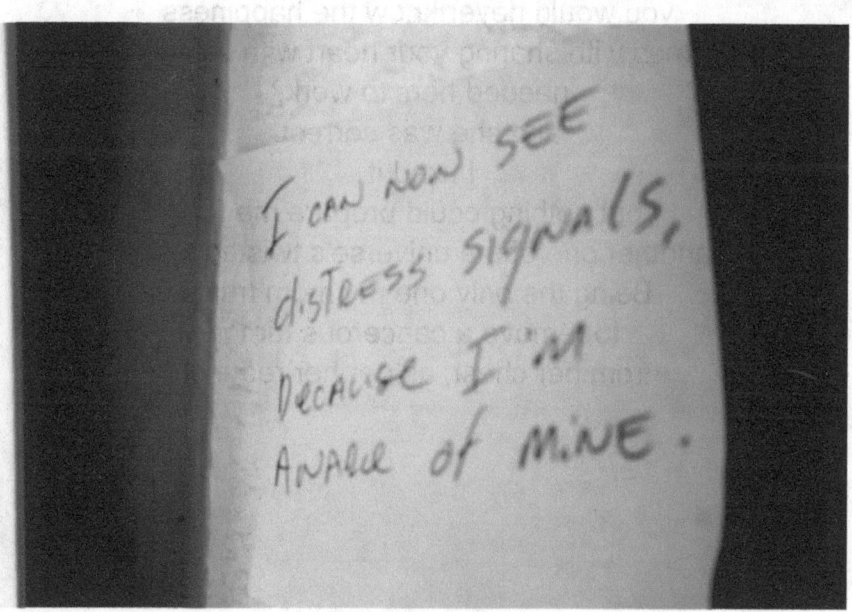

Love Neccessary

A steady surgical hand,
galvanized nerves, empathy, and pride.
I've become conditioned with time,
the loss of life and countless survivors revived,
and happy to be alive.
I'm married to one,
so she reminds me of that.
If it weren't for her
being on the brink of death
("Her words"),
you would never know the happiness
"that comes with sharing your heart with someone who
needed hers to work,"
and she was correct.
I fixed it,
but nothing could prepare me for
another one of the universe's twisted tests.
Being the only one my mom trusts
to remove a cancerous tumor
from her chest, as per her request

Motion of Woes

Looking at a bubbling cup of scorpion stinger,
103% proof that I can escape from life's chafing pain this
way.
My heavenly sphere
is perpetually dingy and chipped concrete gray,
and poison darts rain down to refresh me,
as in refreshing.
The experience of being torn from peace,
the country of grief,
an aerial view of my cracked and trashed
topographical heart.
Tarred rivers of bitterness
could be seen snaking through the terrain.
The fire-water sears my mouth, throat, and mind.
Gremlins turn into angels,
and those who meant me well into demons,
mean as hell.
My tongue unshackled,
a black bile reservoir oozing forward
onto the fragile plains of my relationships.
Staggering with a confident stumble,
blurry plaques hang on the wall of a dimly lit hallway.
With one faint red light to highlight
my wall of shame is in the basement.
My memory lane is paved with roadside bombs,
shrapnel missing me,
but ripping through everyone in my care-a-van.

I have another bubbling cup,
my life skills and liver are utterly shot,
unable to filter
the impurities that I am reintroducing to me.
Woe is me, huh?
Blaming everyone else
with a shaky finger stained with blood.
I look at my pure white facade of self-righteousness,
and it's smeared, soiled, and stained.
Who was the murderer of my dreams?
Woe... it was me!

My Gift

I don't want to persuade anyone to believe me.
I prefer walking out what I eloquently express,
tasting the proof that's in the pudding.
This is what I can offer the world after leaving.
Hopefully, I can inspire men to remove
the pistol from their mouth,
stop the razor from digging deeper into their wrists,
remove pills from their fists,
take their neck out of the rope, and help them step down
from the stool
they were going to jump from.
For I know what it feels like to be insatiably empty,
with nothing left but death seeming like my best interest.
In misery, feeling apathetically downtrodden,
looking out into the world as if I don't belong in it.
From this, I learned that tears lubricate
the ability to visualize yourself in a better light
while crawling from a benchmark poverty line.
We can still smile; pain prompts action to survive.
I love who I have become instead of putting
myself through redundant corporal punishment.
A nine-tail whipping from my own bad decisions,
screwing myself over and over like having recurring
wet dreams with a succubus.
I'll give back good vibes while navigating through
the world optimally conscious, speaking truthfully

with a sound mind,
without discordant harmonics.
I found that being present is good soul medicine.
So, being present with people and not entertaining
future themes about who's before me,
but rather giving a gift worth giving, being attentive.
I'm addicted to being "him,"
a model that stays golden.
"BVOM"—best version of myself,
sobriety as a safe holding.
While examining the hairless patches and dirty adhesive
residue from me ripping off
the sticky label society placed on me,
sent off a dissertation on my cognitive distortions
via email and a backup copy through snail mail.
While my pain fills the inkwell of my pinned essay:
"Think well; winning thoughts versus those that fail."
I found it practical to change my city statues
on statutes of thinking black men,
creating the first of a few disproportionate memorials
of him sitting in reflection, locks hanging, book in his hand,
with an engraved title of
"Knowledge with action with focus is power.

Our Own Stuff

They say if you don't stand for something,
you will fall for anything,
but some will stand for anything
just to save themselves from falling.
We have been selectively dividing our attention
and what we should be conscious of,
like having the gleaming guilty pleasure
of owning blood diamonds.
We are loud and boisterous when confronting opponents of
us,
but silent when the boy distributes rat poison among us.
You could hustle,
but what if your hustle brings destruction to us?
True value misunderstood due to a focus on victimhood.
Stories of recycled trauma,
conditioned into reminders,
converting Freedom Fighters into grievance writers.
Mourning through our Twitter fingers about injustice,
but bullets have never been just to us.
Scroll once,
a new rapper's murder is trending,
had a record called "Pull Up, Pull Up."
Shadow dialogue from those in the fog,
substance lost.
Molesting fragile minds with
nose candy, syrup, and burners.
Our subcultural staple

contributes to wanted-for-murder posters
being stapled.
Clinton's aforementioned super predators.
Color-coordinated gang, gang.
Catching a body is a badge of honor,
forgotten the morals of Big Mama.
Face blown away for a chain.
Our life expectancy is worse than
when we used to hang.
Ignoring our self-inflicted communal sickness,
that's like chopping off our leg
when we have a heart condition.
We got work that needs to be done
that only we could do.
But this is going to require us to look
critically at our own stuff

Park Impressions

Hearing the tic tic tic of blurred
swirling double dutch lines.
My little cousin's female initiation games
of eye, feet, and rhythm coordination.
They both hate and love when I try to jump in, paradoxically.
The smell of seared beef tips hugging charred
mesquite smoke possesses my nose.
The water nozzle quells the raging
neon red embers of charcoal,
eyes stinging happily as belly slopes
and grumbles with Miller High Life,
eardrums greeted with
deeply conditioned soul tunes.
I believe it was heard before in my mother's womb:
"What's going on, what's going on
what's going on, what's going on
Ooh! Ah a Ah
"We need some loving here today."
I told y'all to stop kicking this damn ball over here!
The kids twice warned, but only nodding
their heads with slurpy and soda sugar-crazed eyes,
so that they could resume
their "pre-tablet era" impromptu:
Creative cardio games, freeze tag you're it,
Christine! Bolt them doors! Tenna Henna!
Nick, don't cut! We ain't playing fives!
Black and white dots slammed,

vehement domino proclamations
among tipsy uncles.
My great auntie's scarlet lipstick
signature still resting on her personalized
canvas of my face.
Regardless of how old I am,
she remains faithful to our tradition.
This right cheek is hers,
my wife has to understand.
....It's too early for firecrackers.
Pop, pop-pop-pop-pop-pop.
Everyone stops in the park,
frozen like a flash mob under a
synchronized watch.
Nobody shot, it was over a few blocks.
Life resumes for us,
paper plates splashed with pork 'n beans,
chicken thighs and links,
spring field sodas cracked,
shooing away the bees.

The Preist At The Gallows

With weary eyes and parched lips,
I mutter a small prayer and kiss the crucifix
for the condemned men I see before me.
The irony of it,
kissing an instrument of death in order
to bless those who are entering another phase of it.
Shush, all these damned souls.
The ones that are to be hanged,
and the onlookers who were
just good enough
to hide their guilt from the prying eyes of the law.
You know, the secretly guilty among us.
The masses gathered here today,
sneering and pointing in judgment.
Spectators with hypocritical logs hanging out of their own
eyes.
I sigh as the stares of condemned men's eyes vary:
fear, sorrow, anger, disgust, resilience, weariness,
and sometimes, yes even sometimes, relief.
I suppose this is when men are at
their truest selves.
When they have no more time left
and just the rest of themselves to give.
The dust blown to and fro
is a reminder of how temporary our
existence is here.
Gone in a twinkling of an eye.

Although we could never freeze smoke,
we could observe it while we can.
See... Gone.
Would you like to confess your sins before
departing this world and into eternity, my child?
I ask while secretly doubting
that God will forgive a wicked person
who lived his whole life abominably
and, in seeing his own impending doom,
chooses to finally
confess that he was wrong.
Just to manipulate his way into heaven.
But!... Sigh... if only I could help them
through their final traumas of death.
Then I would be a hope for even the most
vile of men, because, for at least one moment
in our lives,
we were all one of them.
This leads me to question myself.
Do I serve God just to avoid hellfire?
And if He knew that,
would heaven be granted to one that doesn't
necessarily love Him for who He is?
To save my own skin from melting over and over again?
Or
when a man pleads with his last waking breath
that he's innocent,

and it's something in my spirit
that knows it's true,
yet I still offer him a confession,
as if his soul is corrupt.
Yet he is the victim in this,
but still, give him the treatment of the condemned.
Would God have preferred for me to fight
for this man instead
or even take his place?
Just as the body goes through the dark passage
of the gallows floor,
we too will pass from this life to the next.
The difference is that
I know there is dirt and a corpse
down there at the end of that line.
But even I have my doubts
about what awaits us beyond
the door of a stopped heartbeat.
God bless us all.

Reflective Coin

A jasmine perfume whiff of wind
takes me by the hand to memories of my youth.
Carousels and popcorn,
I could not afford but my mom's embrace
was a luxury in itself.
Only half of me saw it that way, though.
The other half stole,
just to be able to temporarily
gratify me.
Only to miss it a minute later.
The seashells at the beach and cotton candy.
I had enough change for just one
play at the arcade,
the rest of the time, I watched others' enjoyment
and was sometimes lucky when
coins were found,
when I scavenged the slots
of previously played games.
Poverty gave me opportunities
to wonder about the foreign realm of financial freedom.
If only I could say when I was younger
I felt this way, but
lest one become like a child
he cannot enter the kingdom of God.
I am now a middle-aged man,
still wondering about financial freedom,
not for the inflation of vanity in my life,

but to do what I want to do most,
change lives and bring smiles to
the downtrodden whose feet hurt
from walking in circles too long
along the miracle mile.

Smiles of Symbolism

The smile can be
the gesture an assassin uses before she places the bullet.
It could be the beginning of a lifelong romance
with generational consequences.
It could be a shield against prying eyes
that are either honestly concerned about your emotional well-
being
or those that use your woes as poking centers.
A smile can be a photographic staple
even when a family is in the midst of a storm.
It is used to show happiness,
now just a portrait of the smiling family doppelganger
hangs in the living room,
staring down at the feuding bunch.
It could be the byproduct of vengeance fulfilled
or the mark of one being proud
of the years of training that
accumulate into accomplishment.
"That's my baby!"
It could be a sign of bearing someone else's humiliation or
preventing them from feeling further embarrassment.
It could be used to show a sign of being supportive,
a smiling display: "Oh, that's okay."
It could be a bully's nonverbal punch
or a bully-beater's reward for living up to his name.
What would the world be without it?
Let's see: ummm...
every emotion enjoyed like a
photo pose from the 1900s---stoic.

Soul Sore

Sometimes I...
feel like I'm...
playing a full clip game of
ghetto roulette
with the bastard sons of broken mental slaves,
nibbling to death
on the Achilles heel of their brothers' forward progress.
They're trying to reattach broken shackles,
and took a welding class just for that,
with a coward's degree in innuendo combat.
I mean shoulder to shoulder,
close-quarter cutthroat,
from friends the closest who say they love you the most,
stabbing you with a rusty and serrated blade of broken trust,
giving you the blues over dark clouds
of simple grays,
can't stand the rain yet soaked up.
Hating with jaded love,
amor de carne,
fang smiles,
frienemy memorabilia,
thickened blood pumping from heartache.
Their loyalty was trash,
memoirs from a city dump.
In the hint of words, an odd mix occurs:
one tablespoon of "you my n****,"
one ounce of "trust nobody,"

and a gallon of "I don't give a f*** about s***,"
and stir.
Now pour... and down it.
Irrational envy gets you drunk,
on the balcony tipsy.
Shhh... sometimes it will be your own kind.
If someone could have only told Malcolm and Nipsey—you
see,
the roosters come home to roost,
and pit bulls occasionally lock on their pups.
Disillusioned that God only hears you,
well here's a command that should
keep you company:
"Thou shalt knock off the f******,"
and your false appearance of truth.
And that's what's up.
You see, actively avoid those that
prefer to walk in superstition
instead of running to claim their birthright,
faith inactive or used impractically,
oddly speaking b******* over their life,
then knocking on wood infested with termites.
I can tell they hate themselves,
and could smell the disease of disbelief
seeping through their pores,
trying to tear down everything around you,
thoughts misconstrued

like a dilapidated psych ward.
Saying "you gonna fail at everything you do."
Psst. I shook my head, closed my eyes,
and deflated the importance of you
and this conversation... for with you,
I can't disagree more.
Don't be distracted by the circus,
be concerned with the undercurrent.
You can have bloody rivers
running through green pastures,
gentle breezes carrying lethal gasses,
penthouse vista views overlooking the bottomless pit,
we're cursed with being surface
and misappropriating our purpose.

Stop Breath Release

I want to release this vise-gripped stress
that has "boa" constricted
on my ability to find rest.
Standing still, yet heartthrobs,
shoulders and knots for the peace I have not.
I've been cheating on my well-being,
having an affair with a miss-stress,
that has been poisoning me slow,
with thinking the worst
and acting out of my best interest.
My mind has been the honeycomb
hideout for hostile squatters,
defecation graffiti artists hence the stinking thinking and s*****
preponderances.
Wrestling with future events
that I can do nothing about today,
emotionally power bombing myself
through a glass table from the top of a steel cage.
My unblinking eyes pried wide in a day-mare,
not responding to snapped fingers or hand waves across my
face,
not glad to be here
in this haunted house-like mental space.
I've turned an oasis into a torture chamber,
cup not half full but cracked, dry, and broken in a landfill.
Its neighbors are bodies of the versions of myself
I missed out on becoming.

If only I would have stayed still and embraced wise moments,

obsessed with controlling the things I can't,
yet fearful of the things I can.
While presently eating out of post-apocalyptic pork and bean
cans,
thinking of the fallout from disasters I can only imagine could
occur,
super gluing my cheeks into a smile with responses that are
well rehearsed.
How you doing?
I'm good, blessed… seeping from my face, knowing that
nothing about
how I'm feeling is truly okay.
Creating my own demons that chase and scratch me in my
sleep,
visualizing people rejecting me before they even have the
chance to,
putting words in their mouth,
expressions on their face,
exaggerating their violent nature,
filling in their intentions and plans too.
Painting in my mind what I think they should
think about me,
somewhere between un and flattering,
but it's really me,
all the hyper precautionary tales my mind weaves.
I may need to just stop, breathe, release.

Peace Shot

Maneuver for the 3,
transitioning my mental imagery,
channeling Jordan, Curry, and Kobe
after 2 crossovers.
I exhale and shoot through
the outstretched palms of
my defender.
A desperate man.
My wrist flicks, ball clean through the rim.
Swish.
There's silence.
Seeing that it's only me,
rusty backboard, concrete, and a dream.
Even though the whole world is asleep,
I'm still a winner to me.

Phoniex Trials

Organized dismay,
radar pinging half-truths,
confusion is intentionally set forth to set you backward,
well, moonwalk while you're doing so.
Gracefully twirl with the whirlwinds of chaos,
and when the earth trembles beneath your feet,
enjoy the full body massage,
viewing pain as necessary for growth,
soil for your dreams,
sunlight for your leaves.
When peace leaves, it makes you miss it that much more
when it returns.
The plight of a black swan,
black sheep-ed for being judged on her process
of transfiguring into greatness.
Everybody likes to look at the fruit of the tree
but not the roots sprouting from the soil seed.
The ashes are stirring, and form is emerging,
while small embers illuminate the eyes
of this rising phoenix.
Chains of doubt, criticism, and mockery melting away
from the neck of someone no longer enslaved
to other people's opinions.
Self-love recaptured from the sadistic hands of self-pity,
sweat on the warrior's brow
from the marathon miles
endured with delight.

Spectators view them with angst
and borderline dismay,
seeing only agonizing tribulation,
while the athlete's internal victories are always celebrated.
This is where it counts the most.

Strength to Draw From

As long as my heart beats,
even with teary eyes,
I will read notes on the symphony lines
this life has composed for me.
Looking on to others for an example of perseverance,
emerging as victors from
victims of circumstance,
with a sandpapered paper tongue I pant.
Concentration camps - branded, cursed, card stamped.
Slave ships to plantations - branded, cursed,
card stamped.
Dodging bullets and arrest from border patrol,
fleeing drug-smuggling gunmen and political corruption,
just to be kissed by Diablo de Americano.
Green card scrapped,
to being here and dodging bullets
from gang rivalries, arrested, beaten by police, bleeding.
Pol f*** s***, drowned by
but my country tisivi,
but my body floats - Damn.
While the desert scorches the feet of refugees
deserted by the world.
Abandoned cake for dessert,
but refusing to release their
bulletproof peace.
Although what they once considered home
is now war-torn.

Capsized boats equal watery graves.
Hundreds of thousands times ten displaced,
looking to the sky for hope, but all
they see are drones.
Trying to survive the horrors before them,
extracting glory from the gruesome.
War-inflicted amputee, teaching his son
how to do push-ups.
A young girl born with no hands
perfecting cursive writing,
a swift kick in the ass for my
chicken scratch
or for being idle and twiddling my thumbs.
A woman with her breast removed,
hair loss chemo, refusing to lose
the beauty of showing the world
the beauty of the struggle
and how to give the best hugs.
Pink ribbons and prayer circles,
this is just an exemplary form of perseverance
as it appears to me.

The Drift

I haven't seen the earth in a week,
my lips painfully split
when I speak.
Can't afford to be pissed off, sick from the sea,
thirst only satisfied through water bottles filled
with the fluid from my struggling kidneys.
Even though there's a body of water around me,
it's obstructed
by the view of 25 bodies from this view of counting,
diseased are 3,
and our navigator can no longer be trusted,
it means we are lost.
I'm hungry,
but I can never feast on a little one
that was so full of life just a week ago.
The others say it's for survival
and "better us eat
than the sharks."
The mother insisted again,
raw meat in her hands,
saying "I give you a part of me so we could have at least a
chance
to make it to the new land."
Not sure to deem it savagery
or the greatest gift she's sacrificing.
A chance at life.
I'm glad she sat beside me.

The Lies I Love to Hate

Tell me you're lying today so that I could be harmed by truth
tomorrow.
Let me know I'm beautiful so that you could hide your
ugliness
from the time of my life you borrowed.
Remind me that I'm strong but don't help me forget I'm
vulnerable.
Show me that you're solid, but I am but a brittle vase
shattered
on your marble floor.
Tell me you know me better than I know myself so I could
never
know you.
Help me pick out a disguise, I mean outfit,
to accentuate my beauty but keep my heart festering with rot.

How I love you so, can never let you go.
A love triangle with me, myself, and I—
jealousy at each corner because one does what the other
won't do, and the other what I wouldn't dare.
An infinity mirror stopped at the third reflection,
cancerous conceit found in all three.
Where does time go when at discourse with self?
As long as you don't answer yourself, they say,
then our open-ended questions are okay.
The storm of the day and I.

The Light in The Tunnel

I see them squinting,
face twisted full of opinion,
mad dogging like they're rabies-stricken.
Trying to muffle and cloak the radiance I evoke,
there's something to be said about shade being thrown
at bright minds.
But why should I apologize for the shine that hurts their eyes?

LEDs work best at night time.
I glow,
from the power stumbled across
during the humble walks of
relinquishing control
over the things that
I don't
and never had hold of.
They want me weak and needy like a pup with parvo,
pleading no contest to things arguably the most.
I have the dignity of she with white jeans,
my essence will bleed out if I go with the flow.
My worldview lens crafted by the father,
I beam as his offspring.
S***, I'm an organic architectural marvel.
Here are some sunglasses; my intensity exhausts thee.
Reining back the dial on my drive
is too much of a hassle,
finally can remove the under-construction signs

from at least one area of my life,
and blow out the vigil candles
of where my old self died.
Yeah, I want the world to see it,
the fruits and my grind,
placed on the pedestal as
a monument of moments, well hours,
I had to toil,
surviving the thoughts
of not believing
I would survive the turmoil.
Why hide the blisters on my palms?
I worked for these,
bringing a weathered texture to my handshake,
evidence that I held on during the storms of life,
while the things that weren't so bolted down got torn away.
You know, the baggage and weight that I thought made me
feel safe,
but if I held on, I would have drowned that day.
Don't underestimate the beauty
forming inside the ugliness of a cocoon.
There's a lot of dream killers out there,
but I'm into the business of bodies being resumed,
those that succumbed to their failures.
Don't just brush it off,
that dirt on your shoulder needs to be vacuumed,
and the surrounding area.
If you're stuck in a slump, it's time to move.
I need company at the top, see you soon.

The Patriot

Long range,
Wind factored in.
.50 cal metal jacket
inserted in the rifle chamber.
The president waves, protesters rave.
He fills his lungs with air and—
exhales.
Finger gently squeezes the trigger
like a toddler's head being put to bed,
down on the pillow.
The sound spits suppressed,
finding its mark,
burrowing a hole in the chest of
the president's would-be assassin.

The Sea In Me

Hey! It's your good ole ocean,
vast, salty, and deep,
at continual motion yet
still, calm, choppy, and rough.
Expanding as far as your eyes could reach,
I am you and you are me,
but there has been a disconnect between us.
So let me let you in on a little something.
See—you were all born from my waters.
It's funny that science and religion
bicker and argue
over whom or what gave birth to you.
Well, I'll say it true:
In the beginning,
I was that primordial soup,
an earlier version of me
from which everything that breathes sprang.
But I was crafted and fashioned by something,
a force, a process, intelligence.
Yep, what you call God created me
and threw all this into play.
So there you go, debate solved.
Have a good day.
Anyway… you know,
you and I are more alike than not.
When I get cold,
my waters can be unforgiving.

I harden myself to the world
in the form of jagged icy rocks,
and I'm not easily gotten through to,
just like you.
I could appear smooth on the surface
but have dangerous undercurrents,
just like you.
With pleasant smiles
yet inwardly disturbed and hurting.
Yep, I've been in toxic relationships too!
"All those bruises will heal,
she loves me too much to leave.
She's not going anywhere."
Ring a bell? Ding ding!
For me, it's chemical and oil spills,
environmental abuses.
But oh, I'll clean it up over time, y'all say.
It ain't hurting nothing, I'll always be here, it ain't going
nowhere.
Y'all know how people subjectively view me
could range from peaceful and serene
to upset, vengeful, or deadly.
I guess it depends on where you're standing.
Your heart beats theme: "Pleasures or Problems."
But I'm just me... I just exist.
I have no intentions—something we
don't have in common.

Y'all say I swallowed everything from planes, boats,
cities, and refugee babies.
For too long I've been
the scapegoat for humanity's errors.
Yep, as a species you could do better.
Most of ya only have a surface understanding of my seas.
That only speaks to how hollow,
surface people are on the surface.
If only you would explore our depths and trenches,
maybe you will find unspeakable jewels,
discover lost wonders
of your unique life.
Uncover graves of former trespasses, accidents, and battles
not to be mourned for but,
rather learned from.
Not to be ashamed of but,
changed from.
Yep, change is good.
I change—evaporate and drift to the sky
until it's time to rain,
soak in soil, to flow through your veins.
Whether tears of pain or joy,
they taste the same, huh?
Be water, my friend,
don't forget where you came from.

The Circle of Life

Falling from death-defying heights,
extending a referendum to abhor
whatever scandal
the scandalous is composed of.
My composure
remains the same, not one muscle twitched,
not one eyelash flicked.
Wrestling with life
has made me a stone mannequin,
a man that can be unmoved from his views.
Necessarily stubborn.
When hope arrives, I immobilize,
boogie boarding through the shifting tides,
sponsored by a hurricane's eye.
My title championed by
a butcher's exacto blade,
severing my cancerous, haphazard,
half-backward, and inaccurately answered ways.
I turn the page
and find it sprayed with pelleted pinpoints
from the black hole of the gauge.
I could gauge
things seen once and measured twice,
roll the dice and divide the garments
of a Christ mind.
The Divine wrapped within flesh,
and flesh held together by atoms,

83

and atoms by subatomic particles,
partially because the
descendants of
thought are always washed away
by the deluge of the delusional.
Unused thinking
reaching down to earth in which it doesn't belong,
dethroned, deboned, and filleted
to optimal shape and seasoned for taste.

Light House Duty

Lighthouse duty helped me find myself
from my own torrential storms and sea salt-filled lungs.
I was being strangled by the rope of lack of hope,
a queued interlude for healthy vicissitudes.

My laughter was really just a very well-disguised death
gurgle.
Glad to be sober with a revived mind
instead of my purpose and potential torn in two.

I didn't know I needed this,
I've been with festering wounds for so long
I made them fashionable.
Enabled by society's slogan of
"Toxicity is The New Normal."

Thought I had good footing on solid ground
until an earthquake brought down my tower of
disillusionment.
My inner man's ashen hand
twitching out from the twisted
rebar and collapsed concrete.

I can now see distress signals,
because I became aware of mine.
Have you ever seen someone drowning with a smile on their
face?

That was me at one time.

Contemplating my immortality.
This ocean, this lighthouse, these breaker stones
were here before I viewed them,
but I would like to think I was somewhere prior to these.

Not fearing the living while dying paradox
of my life cycle.
Every time I excel, eternity becomes more vibrant,
my present fading to the past when I blink.

Everything new becomes old before you can say "new."
Go through trials and pain to reach paradise?
Being the fittest to survive just to die?
I would love to see the movie of life from beginning to
endgame.

Observing my shadow's silhouette as the sun sets.
"Who is that man?"
The shadow says and I flinch.
"Who, me? I'm just getting around to finding out."

Reconfiguring myself in the soup of my cocoon
with good karmic gestures,
trickle-down blessings,
and positive butterfly effects that ripple.

This Wall Could Talk

I reach over hills, deserts,
cut through rivers, mountains,
section off seas,
and I'm most solid
in the minds of those that mind
if I exist or not.
I am a physical representation of someone else's imaginary
line,
composed of barbed wire, metal fencing,
and concrete that divides,
separating and declaring turf
that's dichotomized.
They say, "This is yours and this is mine,"
even though it was formerly yours,
but war is war.
I killed more, so you have to go.
You're an alien, not native anymore.
I've seen
weary souls traveling hundreds of miles
with blistered feet and swollen expectations,
only to have both rupture
at the now-embrasive sight of me,
a paradoxical object of liberty.
I'm in the industry of
legalized cultural segregation,
when it seems like I've been assigned
as the world's corridor to the land of the free,

to exercise hatred after miles of cold shoulders.
I receive you with open arms, razor wire hugs,
pistols, pat-downs, and turnarounds,
you know, the basics.
I am a protector, divider, or repressor,
a canvas for art, political tool, prison wall, savior, or symbol of
exclusivity?
I guess I have multiple personalities.
When you look at me, what do you see?
What do you think life would be without me?
Would you miss me and want me back if not having a border
turns bad?

Travel Thoughts

The world before me, providing narratives
I would have thought about writing or even dared to.
A long way from home,
meaning leaving my comfort zone.
Airplane mode charged to roam in foreign places,
facing it basically with an adventurous spirit.
Life of the timid, avoiding traffic collisions.
I gave myself permission to live.
These egg shells will have to be without my feet.
My anxiety will have to take the back seat today because
you know what?
I feel like driving—
not drunk this time, but in the right mind,
aware of the precious cargo on board.
To war I went with wasted time spent and vowed not again
to waste any more,
either always being productive or resting
to be productive again.
Severing the hands of my self-saboteur
that proposed phantom opportunities.

Treatment

Open wounds fester emotionally,
103 proof alcohol sanitation taken orally.

It doesn't stop the bleeding,
apply the pressure of acting like everything's okay.

Denial is a psychological antibiotic,
but harsh truths are resistant strains.

The disease is spreading.
Decisions, decisions,
amputation or stagnant acceptance?

One leg in, one leg out of becoming
the best version of myself.
Is it foolish of me to have to decide which leg has to go?

The obvious isn't always so.
Faith and doubt run on the same engine.

To the chopping block!
Use a Civil War bone saw for effect!

I need to feel it.... no anesthetic.
Because I've been numb for a long time.

The old path is behind me,

no prosthetic needed for straddling the fence.

I already fell face first
into the pastures of sobriety.

TugBoat

I could distribute facts
or spew deception.
Tasting the fruit juices of truth
and at the same time
candy that lies are coated with,
altering your perception.
I could encourage a soul
or bury a nation,
bring forth a peace of mind
or furnish it with vexation via statements.
I could flatter needlessly and babble senselessly,
or move in patience,
with a well-tailored response
on the basis of need be.
Misdirect with disbelief or tease, la la la,
stir to climatic ecstasy
between knees.
Who am I?
A tool for the mind?
A motor rotor to manifest thoughts?
A slave to the will of the spirit?
A scapegoat that you suddenly can't
control... I was only told to go?
What great power I supposedly hold,
life and death.
Right... You can't blame me for the
intentions you and only you own.

Live From The Trenches

Words can't describe the feeling
that rocks your soul
when you arrive at a scene
and see
a little girl lying dead
with half of her face
missing.
Clutching her baby doll
with a death grip,
it does something
to you.
What animals could do something
like this?
I guess an angry sorrow possesses you,
but... it's suppressed because you
got to hold your shit.
Be professional and not let
the corpse of this little colored girl
get the best of you.
I see the worst of what
society has to offer,
the underbelly of social pleasantries.
This little girl...
What they call stray bullets,
I call hate bullets.
Last week was a pregnant woman
just sitting in her car, waiting

93

for her sister to come out
to take her to get fitted for prom.
I arrive at the scene
and there's fif... fif,...
fifteen holes in the car,
se... se... seven in that young lady
with two... in her... stomach.
I guess her brother had gang ties
and well...
it's a war out here and them folks is dropping like flies.
You have kids running around with military-grade assault
rifles,
with hundred-drum clips,
waving them on their
Facebook and Instagram.
They have a social murder culture
from my point of view.
It's like they are either in denial
or too traumatized to see their own
self-destruction.
I mean it really baffles me.
One of ours shoots one of them
unjustly and yeah, not saying that's right,
but the nation goes into an uproar,
there's protests nationwide.
People on bullhorns, celebrities coming forward,
but when it comes to this little girl
and countless others
getting shot up like a damn
firing range target,
you don't hear a fucking peep!
They even make music about them

slaughtering each other
and it's played on the radio.
Everybody dancing to murder music,
but what do I know, I'm
just a pig on the beat,
sworn to serve and protect
but it sure is hard these days.
Mothers are losing their boys every day
and I'm the one that has to
knock on their door,
to tell them the bad news.
They all think I'm lying at first,
like they're on a pretty messed-up prank show.
Then comes the stare as if
they're scanning your face for truth.
Then those same eyes begin to pool,
and then it's the soul-piercing screams
that you never quite get used to, and at that moment,
you wish you could bring their child back
just to make their agony stop.
I often say it will be okay,
but, at that moment... it's not.
Nor will it ever be.
You know when I hear Black Lives Matter,
I'm not sure who they are trying to convince.
Their idols are celebrity dealers and murderers,
so they technically celebrate
poisoners and executioners.
They live in fear in their neighborhoods
but are fearless when mobbed,
against the government or us.
Yet they are afraid of saying

anything about shooters and drug dealers
in their community.
I saw a poisoned squirrel the other day,
it's a sad thing to see.
It runs in circles, crashes into walls,
and completely oblivious to predators.
That's how I've been seeing
these kids nowadays,
just... just... gone on every drug imaginable.
I got spat on the other day
by a protester,
a young lady yelling at the top of her lungs with
searing rage, screaming "Fuck the Police!"
"We want Justice!"
I guess she didn't remember me,
Nope, but I remember her.
Her brother, a promising college student,
gunned down in a drive-by.
He couldn't breathe,
they couldn't stop the bleeding.
Everybody saw the shooter,
but nobody wanted to say nothing.
We figured it out,
brought her brother's killer to justice.
She thanked us then,
but now she's cursing us
because of a few dumb-asses
mishandled that Floyd situation.
Well, it's damned if we do,
damned if we don't.
I mean,
if we completely remove ourselves

from their community,
you will see unimaginable horrors.
Trust and believe there's more
demons than angels
in those neighborhoods.
You think the bloodshed is pooling now?
With no police presence
there will be rivers,
a drastic drop in the black population
from their own hands.
From what I see daily on the job,
it seems they
hate each other more than
any racist ever could.
They make tree lynching look like
childish play out here in these streets.
If you ever want to know if a people are ill,
just count the kills.
But what do I know?
Just a white guy
reporting from the front lines,
but at the same time working from the outside in.

Where I'm From

I'm from ammonia, bleach fumes, and Boric acid,
cleanliness is next to being roach-free.
I'm from a home being the happiest on the 1st and 15th.
I'm from the projects,
the largest known social project pending.
I'm from tempered love,
hot out of the furnace of struggle,
greasy ovens
with no blue flames because of overdue bills balanced at
dimes of dozens.
I am from second-hand clothing,
swap meet off-brand baby
with emphasized lessons by moms on self-worth
over fashion embroidery.
I am from "do not cross,"
"Thou shalt not,"
"why not," and
"who makes the laws anyway?"
I'm from cigarette-burned carpets and three-hour action figure
clanging,
explosions made by my mouth,
and imaginative characters' backstory and dialogue,
these plastic men were my escape.
I am from jazz, oldies but goodies,
public school instruments,
trumpets and wind-blown bullet hole house flutes.
I am from a mother's warmth and a father's distant cold

presence,
but can't judge the temperature of his intention.
I am from a super glue shelter of a broken home.

PICK A SIDE

Play-Doh social constructions,
children role-playing with
weaponized pens of legislation.
What's the difference between
the puppeteers and their toys?
Only one cares about the other's capability to function.
So it is with the government and its people,
I mean zombies,
I mean cattle,
I mean citizens,
I mean Patriots, Dems, Republicans,
damn it, you know what I mean.
Those that are ideologically obese,
fueled by fast food
"let me think for you" propaganda
that the media hands you,
interfering with the election of your own reason-induced
discernment,
weighing all the options considering all the facts.
And not just kernels, but whole truths,
you're only of use if you
think how they want you to... truth.
Screaming about rights
when the only concern is to be right,
willing to bear the teeth of your commitment
for a good week
before the t-shirts, walking shoes, and "you can't do this to

me,
I'm free" posters are placed back in the garage,
great way to compartmentalize.
Sunday for God,
Monday for complaining that it's Monday,
Tuesday for thanking God.
Kill or be killed,
"Thou shalt not kill,"
do what I say, not what I do,
even if you do what I say while doing what I do out of view.
Obey the laws of the land,
but break them in order to change them.
Maaaaaan.

Haiku Stream

Dreams, smoke, and mirrors,
inhale reflections of hope,
sleepwalking awake.

Shock of cold water,
spider web tension of time,
stream of awareness.

Pinch me - sign of life.
Numb the pain of the gesture,
appreciate it.

Breath, animate self.
Suffocation is idle.
Exhale and repeat.

Box, bullet, chamber.
Fear, anger, squeeze, fire, run, toss gun.
Caught, child dead, newspaper.

Love drug to relapse.
Touch withdrawals, affectionate shakes.
Cold without her cure.

Expand, drink, thirst.
Cotton island, lake of flame.
Next time bring water.

Soft kisses over
poisonous conversations.
Razor tongue, silk mouth.

Chemist formula,
pleasure, pain and in between,
like elemental.

Labor, pain, water breaks,
contradictions, birth contract pinned.
Innocence left by guilt.

Life in the bloodline,
one power, diffused essence.
Me and you - us - whole.

Sand bags, floodwater,
swimming cars and trees,
yet drowning in bills.

Love don't love nobody,
therefore I do in spirit.
Join me, see it's true!

Exhaustive mind race,
iron legs of volition.
Moving finish line.

Caterpillar fly.
Baby builds orbit shuttle.
Mind - no - type - think – free.

Warm welcome, cold world.
Conditions of peace and hardship.
Fine print magnified.

Truth, blind braille outcomes.
Feel what you refuse to see.
Perception's texture.

Figure eight sideways,
life cycle continuum.
Enjoy the current.

Burnt leaves clothed spirit.
Turtle shell necklace on rope.
Swing confident - brave.

Locked in gold solder.
Cipher etched - "Wisdom Loves Mind."
Seasons apparent.

Quickening vital stride,
drummer praised under pressure.
Pre-enslavement.

Death sanitizes wealth.
Love and hate are rivals.
For sale and for free.

Blessed hands caught grief first.
God sent, I man, faithful change.
Blessed eyes see marvels.

Village born true love,
set your gaze attentively.
Fight hell and win hope.

Gray paint, flowers, grave.
Detachment, worth a loose grasp.
Wet map can't find home.

Two steps to freedom.
Corns and bunions ache so bad.
I'll dance anyway.

A miracle mile,
or an accursed marathon?
Neutral finish line?

Rug burns from prayer.
Throat sore from yelling at air.
The kingdom's within.

Moist lips on big-stick,
ice cream trucks sell crack too.
Dry lips on glass pipe.

Drunk, inflamed with faith.
Blind devotion, soulless eyes.
Suicide bomber.

A wave of guilt flows,
self-forgiveness my surfboard.
I'll crash then surf on.

American Hue

Eyes bloodshot,
scarred yet gratefully sweating,
it's hot!
Mind stewing over America's melting pot!
Sip the culture broth.
A social primordial soup of tribalism
and an attempted understanding of each other's idolistic
views.
In a room where a belly belches, fragrant rot
from ills digested,
hatred constructs taught.
A malformation of thought.
Children on playgrounds are living proof
that the madness of prejudice is
force-fed by adults, rust-faded tablespoons.
Harmful, like putting lead in their juice.
We all evolved from monkey bars,
sophisticated primates with different shapes and shades
in which we were made.
Creating false notions of superiority,
and customized gods to favor our justified hate.
Pledging allegiance blindly,
elementary forms of being accustomed to just following.
Don't choose!
Popular opinion is quantified as truth.
The American Dream,
fun house mirrors mazes with murderous masked men,
saying let freedom ring off the neck jangles of bond servants.

Cursed cursive inscribed.
The Bill of Rights. We are but
human poker chips to throw at debt
yet paid for in IOUs.
Purchased by domestic birth,
branded with 7 digits, so that we could feel secure socially
with diminished self-worth.
God bless America.
Veteran battle wounds and tears of widows.
Our security eggshell fragile.
Tight roping in turbulent winds,
with the sprained ankle... illusions of peace.
A star-spangled stability.
As we fluff up and sink
our heads into our memory foam pillows,
when was America ever united?
Division is its hallmark character trait.
We fight and scream for realities we've never seen
as if we are all in sync,
with our definitions of these themes.
Freedom, equality, equity, justice... peace?
Our Lady of Liberty is nursing with breast cancer,
capitalistic freedom of a tumor.
We the consumer,
extending helping hands yet they're gloved with razor blades.

God bless the world of animal stock.
Like reading canker sore lips,
can't help but to notice. Damn!
What more can you take from the have-nots?
A hypothetical loaf of bread

will not fill your belly.
A difference between promises? Said and met.
The word became flesh.
Plymouth Rock atrocities.
Some rocks are to be left unturned.
Skeleton closets... unkept.

The End yet Beginnig.

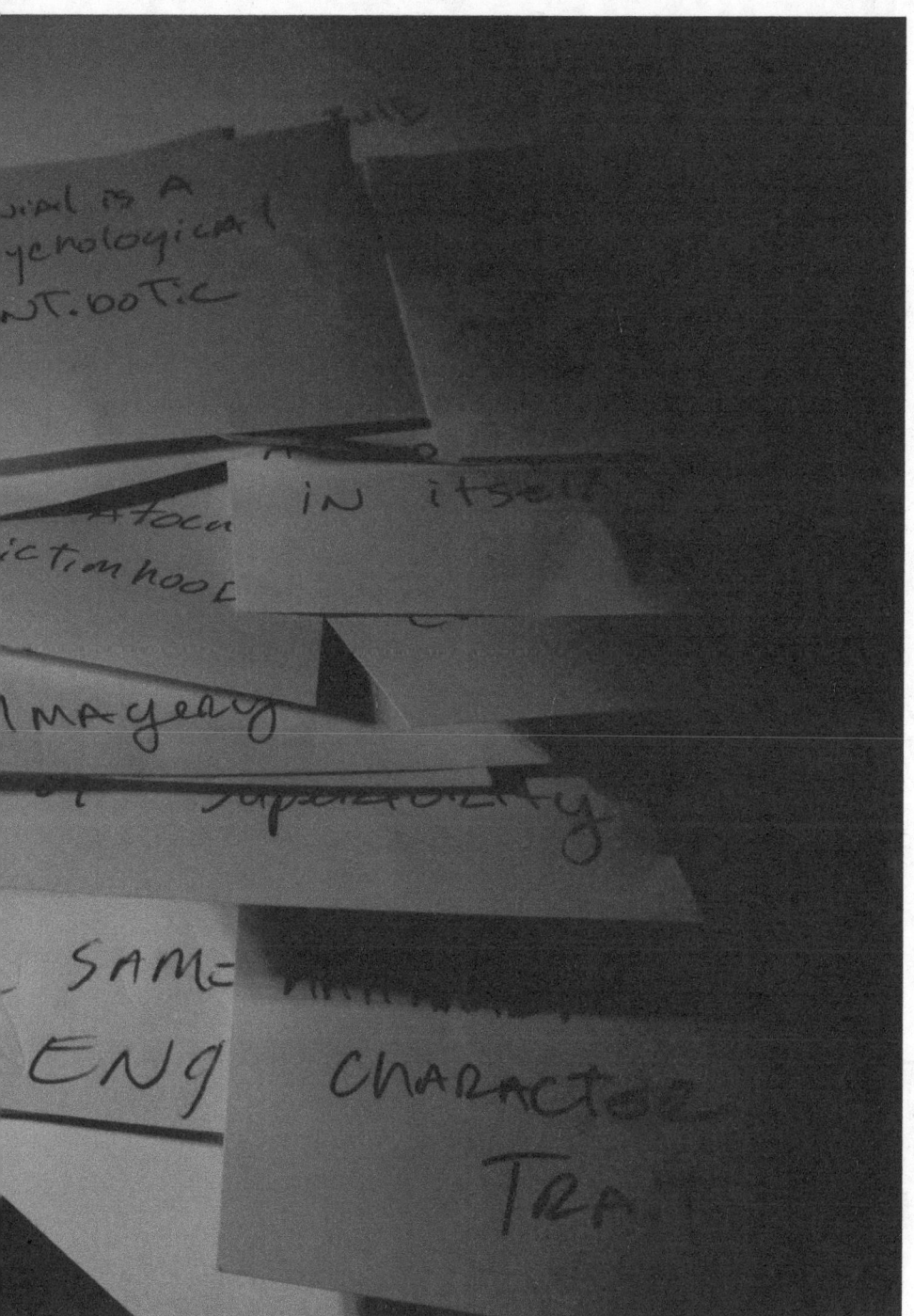